How To Protect Your Child From Bullies

A Practical Guide for Parents

by

Coral Milburn-Curtis

Published by Word4Word, Evesham, UK
ISBN-10 0-9551677-7-9
ISBN-13 978-0-9551677-7-5
Printed and bound by CPI Antony Rowe, Eastbourne

Personal Message from the Author

Every effort is made to maintain the accuracy of this material. If you find any errors or inaccuracies, please let me know immediately. The guide is written in British English, so please accept my apologies if any spellings 'jump off the page' at you.

Rather than refer to 'he/she' or 'him/her' throughout the guide, I have stuck to the use of 'him' and apologise if your child is a girl. I hope that you will still find what I have to offer useful. If you are unsure about undertaking any of the ideas presented in this guide, then you should seek independent advice. There are many further references for you to investigate at the back of the book.

To my children, who taught me all I know

Acknowledgements

The inspiration for this work has come from several sources, but particularly from the many children and parents with whom I have worked over the years. Their courage in overcoming the scourge of bullying has helped me to develop the anti-bullying techniques described in this book.

Thank you to my husband Graeme and my sons Daniel and Andrew for being so tolerant and supportive, for seeing the value of this work and for helping me to find a way to make it a reality.

About the Author

Coral Milburn-Curtis BA, Cert Ed, CPSE, NLPP is an educationalist with experience as a teacher, headteacher, OFSTED inspector, Department of Education team leader, educational consultant, writer and Neuro-Linguistic-Programming practitioner.

Previously the headteacher of the school dubbed the 'Best School in England', for six years in a row, she now specialises in personal development for children.

In addition to giving seminars, presentations and workshops, she writes columns for a number of magazines and internet providers. She lives in Oxfordshire, UK.

Visit Coral online at www.neverbullied.com

Contents

Introduction

Is Your Child Being Bullied?

The thought that your child might be a victim to bullies is every parent's nightmare.

I know the gut-wrenching feeling, the physical pain of leaving a child at the school gates, when you know that your own child is suffering at the hand of others. I know what it's like to have a child desperate not to go to school in the morning and I also know first hand what it's like to be on the receiving end of parents' distress – parents whose families are being destroyed by the pain of watching their children suffer.

For over three decades it has been my mission to use my skills to give parents what they want for their children. In all that time, the first thing parents always say to me is that they want their children to be happy. There is nothing more likely to tear a parent apart than to have the realisation that their child is being bullied. As time has gone on, my work has become more and more focused on helping children who find themselves the victims of bullying. In this book I will share with you some of the tried and tested secrets and techniques which I have found most useful in helping a child to become bully-proof.

A Very Different Approach ...

How is my approach different from the many previous initiatives? It is simple: *How To Protect Your Child From Bullies* focuses on your child, **not on the bully**.

My approach complements and supports the initiatives put forward by major anti-bullying organisations, but it differs fundamentally in one significant aspect. Whereas in all major anti-bullying initiatives the answer has been for the victim to 'tell someone' (has that worked for your child?), my solution goes much further and gets to the heart of why a child is bullied in the first place. It then seeks to redress the imbalance of power between the bully and the victim by raising the victim's self-esteem and inner strength, so that the bully leaves them alone. Furthermore, the programme gives the victim a stock of techniques to deflect the bully's advances and to keep the bully away for good. These are techniques which will remain with the child as he grows up and will become invaluable strategies to cope with bullying in the workplace, in relationships and within peer groups.

Bullies will always be there – sadly. If you attempt to stop the bullying by focusing on the bully, then another one will just fill his place as soon as he's gone. A child who is bullied by one person is likely to be bullied by another.

The secret is not to become a victim in the first place.

Of course, bullies need to be reported and brought to account for their actions – school anti-bullying policies detail this approach very clearly, and all anti-bullying strategies and initiatives make it their mission to eradicate bullying by getting rid of the bully.

But has it worked for your child? Is it getting any better?

Why Have Previous Initiatives Been Unsuccessful?

This is a very significant question, because considerable amounts of time and effort have been pumped into one initiative or another to combat the problem.

The reason for this is that anti-bullying initiatives tend to focus on 'telling someone'. The 'solution' to the problem is then dependent on the recipient of the information doing something effective to stop the bullying. Where bullying takes the form of physical abuse, or obvious and detectable teasing, then effective action will take place only if the organisation is sufficiently strong to confront the bully. But as we all know from the stories of too many children, the information is too often ignored.

The National Bullying Survey of 2006 surveyed 8574 children, parents, teachers and adults in the first six months of 2006 in the largest ever investigation into school bullying in the UK. In the survey, 87% of parents reported that their children had been bullied. Surprisingly, 83% of teachers said that they had not seen bullying at their school. You can read the full survey here: *http://www.bullying.co.uk/nationalsurvey/thenationalbullyingsurvey_results.pdf*

This huge difference suggests that even if the victims are 'telling someone', then the problem is clearly not being addressed.

In the same survey, 74% of parents said that the measures taken by the school did not work; 33% of parents were even worried that bullying might make their children suicidal. 'If we always do what we've always done, then we'll always get what we've always got' – which is why, if we want to get something different, we must re-think our approach.

Clearly, 'just telling someone' isn't working.

Of course, bullies need to be reported and brought to account for their actions, as school anti-bullying policies insist. But bullying, as you have probably experienced with your child, is not just about physically hurting a victim. The most persistent, difficult to trace and difficult to combat is the kind of hurtfulness which includes spreading rumours, exclusion, persuading other children to ignore the victim, stealing and damaging possessions. This kind of bullying demoralises the victim and leaves him powerless. Identifying the bully, flushing him out, dealing with the bullying action, writing policies and initiatives are all necessary, but as you are probably only too aware – it does not stop your child from being bullied again. The answer to combating this kind of bullying lies within the victim himself.

This work draws upon my 35 years of experience as a teacher, headteacher, school inspector, friend, carer, Neuro-Linguistic-Programming practitioner and parent. My strategy is based upon my practical knowledge that the way to support a child who is being bullied is to find out why it is happening to him, to strengthen his self-belief and self-esteem, to give him an armoury of anti-bully skills and strategies and to regard the maintenance of high self-esteem as an essential skill which will serve him throughout his life. Time spent on these strategies will be repaid a thousand-fold – in school, in relationships and in the workplace.

Why are some children bullied and others not? Is there such a thing as a 'natural victim'? If your child falls prey to the bullies, what can you do to stop this? The answer is that if your child has a powerful sense of his self-worth, he will know that he can handle anything and thus he will have nothing to fear. Bullies are generally cowards who will not pick on someone with a high level of self-esteem. They need to control and dominate, often because of a deficit in their own social skills, but in order to control someone they need to find a ready victim. The bully does not have any power of his own – the bully's power is centred within the mind of the victim, with the victim being too intimidated to put up effective resistance. This is why the solution to the problem lies within the victim himself.

This publication is not about why bullies bully – that information has been well documented elsewhere, for instance on the excellent Department of Education parents' websites detailed at the end of this book (where there are hundreds of harrowing stories about children who are persistently being bullied in schools). This practical programme will help your child to ensure that he is equipped to handle every encounter, whether 'nice' or 'nasty'. It assumes that we all encounter bullying of one form or another, and whether or not we can handle this depends upon our own inner resources. The practical steps you must take as soon as you encounter bullying are covered too. But the unhappy fact is that the bully will only pick on someone who already sees himself as a victim. He will not pick on the one who sends the message, 'I am strong and secure, so don't even think about it!' That inner strength is what this programme is about.

This guide will help your child if he:

- ☐ Finds himself victimised, bullied or teased

- ☐ Has a low self-image, leading to underachievement in school

- ☐ Is reluctant to go to school because of friendship problems

It is a practical guide which will give you:

- ☐ A toolkit for building up your child's self-esteem and resistance to bullying

- ☐ Exercises which will strengthen his sense of self-worth and his self-esteem

- ☐ Techniques for handling bullies and meanies

- ☐ Techniques for resisting peer pressure and saying 'No'

- ☐ Help to work out friendship problems, cliques and gossips

- ☐ Forms and letters to assist you in dealing with schools

The rewards of this programme are huge. They can last a lifetime.

They can start straight away.

How To Use This Guide

The format of this guide is very user-friendly, so you can use it in any way you like. There are specific exercises for parents, parents with their children, younger children on their own and older children on their own. The exercises are separate and can be used in any order, and you will find that you return to the exercises which have been particularly effective for your child. Some of the exercises will be more suitable for children of a different age to your child, so if you think that, for any reason, a particular exercise might be inappropriate for the moment, then skip it and come back to it later if you choose. You may wish to read through the whole guide before devising your individual action plan, or just work your way through it, making a note of which exercises work best and which need to be repeated.

Either way, repetition is the key.

Practice will ensure that the techniques detailed in this guide will become part of your child's natural behaviour.

Work together with your child. Don't rush through the exercises – they offer a wonderful opportunity for you to get close to him, to discover the patterns of his thoughts and feelings and to jointly affect the quality of your lives. They will help your child to 'open up' and enable a deeper sense of trust to develop between the two of you. If there is a particular exercise which your child would rather not do, then you might wish to use this as an opportunity to discuss how a different child might react to it and this may bring up other possibilities.

Don't just read it – DO IT!

Try to set a specific time each day to do the exercises – after an afternoon snack, perhaps, when your child is not too tired.

You will be introduced to the concept of affirmations, a very powerful means of influencing subconscious self-talk. Affirmations should be repeated ten times each morning and again each evening, just before sleep, when both of you are relaxed. Hopefully, they will be the last thing he hears before he drops off to sleep.

Try to make the programme a family affair. Encourage older siblings to participate and to demonstrate the effectiveness of the exercises. The whole household can become empowered, reinforcing the messages to the child. Grandparents and carers can also help.

Have fun with the programme. Point out to your child that no-one is perfect and that we are all learning all of the time.

Make sure that you keep a diary. There is a template in the Appendix section of this guide, but you will probably want to use a special book for it. Watch how those thoughts become more positive as the programme progresses. Make notes about how your child reacted to each exercise and how you might have adapted it. Please let us know how this guide works for you. We really want to hear your stories.

Good luck – and we'd love to hear from you.

The email address is: preventbullying@googlemail.com

Bullying

What is Bullying?

Dictionary definition: 'A bully is someone who uses strength or power to hurt or frighten other people'. There are several types of bullying:

- ☐ Physical: including physical harm, kicking, pushing, threatening with weapons, using weapons, hazing (initiation ceremonies, giving the bumps, birthday beatings, etc), having possessions thrown around. **This is used by the bully who uses his strength to hurt people and is the form most common to male bullies.**

- ☐ Verbal: name calling, teasing, using cruel nicknames, racist or sexist comments

- ☐ Criminal: extortion, cyber bullying (mobile phone, email, malicious blogging and instant messaging)

- ☐ Emotional: the insidious kind, including rumour-mongering, manipulation, isolation, ignoring, arguing into submission, the silent treatment, giving the 'evils', having possessions stolen or moved, etc. **This is used by the bully who uses power to frighten people and is the form most commonly used by female bullies.**

Physical bullying is, in a way, easier to deal with. There is tangible evidence of what has been done and the required action is fairly clear. The bully has to be either reported or caught red-handed. Either way, there is clear evidence of what has been going on and the school's anti-bullying policy can and should be put into effect – or indeed there may be reason to involve the police. Most overt bullying, including stealing, physical assault, graffiti, extortion, abusive phone calls and mobile phone abuse, is against the law.

If bullying happens in school, it is the duty of the school to sort it out and to do so quickly.

Verbal and emotional bullying is often even more worrying for many children and for their parents. The bully's aim is to demoralise so that he can exert his power over the victim. The most sensitive children can easily fall victim to this kind of bullying because they are vulnerable targets.

This programme is very helpful for these children, the ones who are persistently made to feel powerless and victimised – and whose voices are often unheard.

Victims of emotional bullying may find it tough to talk about their experiences. They may be paralysed with fear, or just accustomed to keeping their worries to themselves. In this case, it is usually one child's word against another's; it is very difficult to catch the perpetrator red-handed and it is most likely that the victim will be told to 'get over it', 'find somewhere else to play', or 'stop telling tales'. Often the bully will call their 'rights' into play, but will afford the victim none. A female bully will often use tears as a way to gain sympathy and the authorities are often confused by the bully into believing that they are in fact the victims. Teachers often find this sort of situation subtle and so difficult to deal with that they are rendered helpless.

If this happens – and it happens a lot – the victim can learn that adults can't help him anyway.

Most anti-bullying initiatives focus on 'telling someone' as the solution to the problem of bullying, as if telling someone will make it go away. As all parents of bullying victims know, this isn't enough. What is needed is action by the person who has been told and if this doesn't happen, as seems to be the case far too often, then the victim is left vulnerable, alone and disillusioned.

No, what the victim needs is a programme of self-protection so that the bully stays away.

What are the Signs of Bullying?

Most of us have experienced bullying at some time or another. Recent surveys, including the 2006 National Bullying Survey, show that bullying is so prevalent in our society that most of us have been affected by it in some way. We know the feelings of hurt, isolation and fear, of being controlled and subject to the apparent power of another. We may not find it so easy to spot the signs of being bullied in our own children. Indeed, bullying is sometimes so subtle that your child might not even realise that what he is suffering is actually bullying. He might also, for one reason or another, be very good at hiding his feelings. The first sign is usually that the child doesn't want to go to school. Some other pointers can be:

- [ ] becoming uncharacteristically moody or short-tempered
- [ ] anxiety, insecurity, insomnia
- [ ] bedwetting
- [ ] stealing money from a purse at home
- [ ] going off their food
- [ ] having difficulty concentrating
- [ ] trying to stay with a teacher or adult during breaks
- [ ] sudden deterioration in class achievement
- [ ] becoming quiet, withdrawn and uncommunicative
- [ ] showing a lack of respect for others
- [ ] regularly losing dinner money
- [ ] physical signs such as cuts, bruises, torn clothing
- [ ] expressions of violence in writings or drawings

Both boys and girls become involved in verbal bullying; boys are more likely to suffer physical violence, whereas girls tend to use verbal taunts, exclusion and friendship manipulation as their main bullying weapons. There is a difference, however, between bullying and mild occasional teasing. The key word here is 'persistent'. Teasing is bullying if it is persistent.

Many teachers will find it difficult to sort out a bullying situation if it appears to be just a case of 'teasing'. Parents too may be tempted to tell the child to 'just get over it' because it's necessary to be able to cope with teasing – it's all part of our western style of humour, after all.

Teasing happens in a good-humoured way. It is usually done by someone who knows you well and probably cares for you. Usually, you find it funny too – but even if you don't, you usually get over it quickly. Someone who is teased is often able to tease back. However, **teasing becomes bullying** if it causes distress and if it is **persistent** in spite of the distress it is causing. If teasing is done as a means of hurting someone, then it has become bullying.

Many bullies just do not realise the consequences of their actions. They may not necessarily have 'problems' of their own, but are just insensitive to the effect of their teasing. Others, however, use bullying as a means of gaining power over their peers, dominating and hurting others as a means of overcoming their own feelings of powerlessness and frustration. They are frequently very weak and insecure, tending to dislike themselves and needing to exert power over others in order to make themselves feel that they have any worth. They are held down by their own destructive thought patterns and try to drag others down to their level in order to justify their own actions.

Key Points:

- [ ] The child who is most likely to be bullied is one who is very sensitive.
- [ ] In general, a child who is bullied feels like a victim and believes that they have been the target of a hurtful act.
- [ ] Most bullies do it out of a need for power over others. Some just don't realise that their actions are hurtful to others – they are just very insensitive.
- [ ] Some bullies see their actions as a game, focusing on the victim's fear.
- [ ] Boys' and girls' peer groups are very different and give rise to different types of gender-specific bullying.

What are the Effects of Bullying?

Undoubtedly, bullying is damaging to children. Not only can they be physically affected, but it can also affect them socially, emotionally and intellectually. School bullying is responsible for such a high level of unhappiness that for many children, their whole lives are subsequently affected. Bullying is frequently cited as a major underlying cause for school truancy. In the 2006 National Bullying Survey, 60% of the 2160 parents surveyed said that their children had taken time off school because of bullying.

Children who suffer bullying on a long-term basis can develop feelings of powerlessness and hopelessness. They are also more likely to develop psychological illnesses later on. If they do not tell anyone about the bullying, then they also suffer the extra stress of not receiving support and understanding. Children who become victims of bullying are more likely to have their relationships and their careers affected by victimisation too.

Bullying affects whole families. Children who are victimised may find that the pattern is repeated when they become adults.

Key Points:

- ☐ Bullies are people who **persistently** tease, scare, threaten or physically hurt others who are not as strong as they are.
- ☐ Bullying occurs everywhere, not only in the school playground.
- ☐ Sometimes the bully masquerades as the victim's 'friend'.
- ☐ It is necessary to identify why the bully is picking on your child in particular – what is your child doing to make the bully happy?
- ☐ It is important to take action to help your child to understand what is happening to him, how to identify bullying and how to break the cycle.

Is Your Child Being Bullied and Why?

Is your child being bullied? These checklists will help you to find out.

Child Activity

	✓
Are you often scared to join in class activities?	
Do you worry about asking for help?	
Do you spend lunch times or break times alone?	
Do you sometimes feel sad and alone?	
Do you find it difficult to make friends?	✓
Do you find it difficult to start a conversation?	✓
Is it easier to play with younger children?	
Do your friends sometimes boss you around?	✓

Adult Activity

	✓
Are there physical signs of bullying?	
Have possessions been stolen or misplaced?	
Does your child complain about going to school?	
Does your child wet the bed during term time?	
Does he ask you for money to take to school?	
Is your child clingy when you leave him at school?	
Has your child's schoolwork suddenly deteriorated?	
Is your child sad, teary, anxious, withdrawn or secretive?	
Is your child often excluded at lunch times and breaks?	

If two or more boxes have been ticked in each of these tables, then it is possible that it is bullying that is causing your child distress. It is now necessary to find out why.

Why is Your Child Being Bullied?

This section can be painful, but you need to understand why your own child is a target for bullies. You may choose the path of blame and believe that your child was simply 'in the wrong place at the wrong time'. If the attack has only happened once, then this is probably the case. But if the bullying is **persistent**, and if your child is targeted, then you need to consider why this is happening.

Does your child make it easy for the bully? Bullies tend to pick on younger, smaller, weaker or more sensitive children, but they are also lazy and they will continue only if they are getting a result. Bullies tend to have a go at a lot of children, before focusing on those who will react quickly and who will 'reward' the bullying with a reaction. They also tend to be cowards and will quickly move on to a more likely victim if they do not get a reaction.

These are some of the reasons why children are bullied. Check to see which ones may be relevant to your child. Add your own reasons.

	✓		✓
Wrong place at the wrong time		Under-developed for his age	
Physically different		Different race/culture?	
Has learning difficulties		Over-protected	
Is particularly talented		Family problems	
Over-sensitive		Shy	✓
Recently joined the group		Tends to provoke	
Low self-esteem	✓	Wears glasses, braces etc	
Unusual habits, stutter etc		Unusual name	

The odd one out in the above list is 'wrong place at the wrong time'. If a child is attacked in a one-off incident, even if the attack comes from a known bully, then the incident is more of an assault than a bullying incident. An assault needs to be reported immediately, if necessary to the police, and you can expect that it will be dealt with appropriately. The key to recognising bullying is that it is a *persistent* offence. **The reason why the bully continues to upset your child is because it works.**

In order to prevent your child from being bullied, you must strengthen:

- ☐ His personal resources
- ☐ His self-esteem
- ☐ His communication skills
- ☐ His coping strategies

Does your child help the bully?

This may seem like a very strange question, but the truth is that many bullying victims assist the bully by reinforcing the behaviour that the bully is expecting. Your child will be feeding the bully's sense of power if he:

- ☐ Avoids making eye contact
- ☐ Blushes easily
- ☐ Shows that he is upset
- ☐ Over-reacts
- ☐ Displays submissive reactions
- ☐ Blames himself

A child with poor self-esteem is likely to be *inviting* the bully to disrespect him. Furthermore, by *reacting*, he is giving the bully exactly what he wants. The bully will soon work out which taunts are going to get a reaction and which are not.

If your child is bullied, then it is highly likely that he has low self-esteem. The way he is treated is a reflection of how he feels about himself.

What Should You Do?

Having sat down with your child and found out exactly what has been happening, your immediate reaction is likely to be wanting to go straight into school. Try to stay calm. Your child needs you to be stable and supportive, to understand how he feels and to come up with a structured plan of action. Reassure your child that the problem can be sorted, without him being victimised any further. Remember too, that if you haven't previously spotted it, then possibly the teacher may not have either.

Approaching the school need not be a stressful experience if you:

- ☐ Bear in mind that you are all on the same side
- ☐ Approach them in a friendly and non-confrontational manner
- ☐ Ask if the teacher has noticed that your child is isolated or unhappy
- ☐ Ask the teacher how you can work together to sort things out
- ☐ Ask if there are any special arrangements in the school such as 'buddy seats', 'listeners' or learning mentors, who might have a specific role in supporting children who become victim to bullies
- ☐ Encourage the school to try to identify the bullies, so that they can be caught red-handed, rather than have your child accused of telling tales.

If you have a meeting with the headteacher or teacher, it is important to write a letter of confirmation, to show that you expect to be taken seriously. An example letter is available for you to use in the Appendix section at the end of this book.

In order to ensure that the school takes your case seriously, it is a good idea to keep a diary of events. A typical layout is also provided for you in the Appendix.

Dealing with Schools

If your child is being bullied, it is your duty to bring it to the attention of the school. Having been a headteacher for many years, I can also say that the need to work together on this issue is paramount. It is very important that you establish from the beginning that you are all on the same side. If your child is being bullied then you are naturally and understandably upset. You have a right to complain and to expect that the school will act to stop the bullying and ensure that it does not happen again.

Schools are committed to resolving this problem. It is expected that they have an anti-bullying policy which is transparent and available for scrutiny. It will have been sanctioned by the school governors and will be a very significant document in the school.

The policy should detail:

- ☐ Who is in charge of the school's anti-bullying policy
- ☐ What children should do if they are bullied
- ☐ What to expect if they bully someone else in the school
- ☐ Where to get help if they are bullied
- ☐ How to follow up with a complaint if the issue is not dealt with satisfactorily.

However, in order to set up a collaborative relationship then you need to try to tackle the subject in a constructive and non-aggressive way, even though you are probably very emotional by this stage.

It may be that the teachers simply do not know what has been going on. There may be two sides to the story, of which you have not previously been aware. Try not to blame, demand or threaten.

Tips for dealing with schools

- ☐ Make an appointment, rather than rush into school. The teacher or headteacher may be busy on other matters and you need to have plenty of time to resolve the issue.
- ☐ It might be a good idea to script what you intend to say and take some notes in with you. Often the fewer words you use, the more impact you make.
- ☐ Take the diary and any other evidence you have with you.
- ☐ Take a notebook to document what is said and what action is being promised.
- ☐ Be persistent.
- ☐ Ask to see the school's anti-bullying policy and the code of conduct.
- ☐ Ask to see the school's accident book and insist that any injuries are recorded in it.
- ☐ Collaborate as much as possible and only go down the route of complaint if there is no other line of action left.
- ☐ Don't take the situation into your own hands by tackling the bully or his parents.
- ☐ Send your record of the meeting to the headteacher (see the example at the back of the book).
- ☐ Arrange a follow-up meeting to discuss the action taken and the outcomes.
- ☐ Continue to monitor the situation and keep the diary going.
- ☐ Continue to support your child in building up his anti-bullying shield.
- ☐ If the bullying does not stop, inform the headteacher that you are taking matters further.
- ☐ Send a copy of your letters to the Chair of Governors. You can get that address from the school secretary. Don't agree to send the letter to the school. Insist on obtaining the private address. Ask for the bullying problem to be put on the agenda at the next Governors' meeting.
- ☐ Contact your local education authority and find out who is the designated education officer for the school. Send copies of your letters to him/her.

- [ ] Some schools have a policy regarding their responsibility for your child's safety on the way to school. Others argue against it. However, if your child is educated at a school, then he has an obligation to attend – it is not a choice. If he's bullied on the way to school, then the school has a 'duty of care' to keep him safe. If your child is compulsorily wearing a school uniform to and from school, then the school must accept responsibility for this duty of care. Ask to see the school's policy on its 'duty of care' for children travelling to and from the school.
- [ ] If all else fails and you decide to move to another school, then make sure that you look for a caring school with an effective anti-bullying policy. Speak to existing parents and tap into the local grapevine by speaking to the mums and dads who are standing in the playground at the end of the school day.

Finally, if your child is still victimised at the new school, then it is a very good indicator that further action is needed to build up his self-esteem and his assertiveness skills.

If you ultimately choose to educate your child at home, there are support groups and specialist consultants to help you (e.g. www.education-otherwise.org). It may be that all you need is to put some space between the child and the school, and build up his sense of self-worth through success and achievement, before re-joining the mainstream education process at a later stage.

Having taken immediate steps to try to get the school involved, it is now time for you to build up your child's resistance, so that the bully leaves your child alone in future.

The answer is to build an anti-bully 'shield', a re-programming toolkit of strategies to change the way your child sees himself in order to keep the bully away in the first place. The exercises in this guide are proven to work. Work through them again and again with your child until the core of his self-belief is strengthened.

Self-Esteem

Checking Your Child's Self-Esteem

Your child is special – a worthy and lovable being who deserves the best. He has the right to wake up happily each morning, knowing that he is safe and that he can face the day with optimism, looking forward to the rewards and challenges of the day. The following checklists will help you to put into perspective your child's current level of self-esteem. (NB. Never confuse self-esteem with arrogance. Arrogance is an over-evaluation of your worth, while high self-esteem is having a healthy opinion of yourself.)

Adult and Child Activity

Read through this list, saying 'I am' before each word, and score as follows: Almost Never (0); Sometimes (1); Often (2); Almost Always (3)

	score		score		score		score
adventurous	2	kind	3	interesting	2	happy	3
depressed	0	shy	2	lovable	2	lazy	0
intelligent	2	trustworthy	3	funny	2	optimistic	2
sad	1	negative	0	proud	1	positive	2
embarrassed	1	energetic	2	guilty	0	boring	1
self-conscious	1	demanding	0	bullied	0	in control	0
stupid	0	helpless	0	fearful	0	confident	2

How did he score?

Words that scored a 3	Words that scored a 0
trustworthy	depressed guilty
kind	stupid bullied
happy	negative fearful
	helpless lazy
	demanding incontrol

31

Analysing the scores

Look at the list of all the words that scored a 3. This is what your child thinks he is almost always. What does this reveal about his self-image? Does it mean that he has high or low self-esteem? Would you and he like to change any of these? Highlight the ones you would both like to change. Which words do you need to increase from a score of 0 to a score of 3? Write them here:

There were some positive and some negative words in this list. **The next stage of this exercise will reinforce only the positive.** Go through this checklist with your child and agree together which words describe him. You will be surprised at how many you can tick. Add some more positive words of your own.

	✓		✓		✓
lovable	✓	loyal	✓	sensible	✓
kind	✓	loving	✓	friendly	✓
gentle	✓	generous	✓	funny	
free	?	truthful	✓	talented	
careful	✓	thoughtful	✓	curious	✓
patient	✓	trusting	✓	creative	✓
capable	✓	sensitive	✓	playful	✓
determined	✓	tidy		calm	✓
full of energy	✓	positive	✓	cooperative	✓
excited	✓	honest	✓	interested	✓
healthy	✓	joyful	✓	organised	
polite	✓	practical	✓	sense of humour	✓

Now ask your child to highlight any words which he would like to describe him but which don't at the moment.

What did you find out?

You should now have an idea of:

- ☐ Your child's level of self-esteem
- ☐ What he likes about himself (this is a very relevant starter)
- ☐ What qualities he would like to add to his portfolio of self-worth

You may have discovered now that he has some beliefs about himself which need to be changed. The exercises in this guide are designed to do just that.

After looking at the results of the last exercise, write down three beliefs that your child has about himself, and that need to be changed:

Self esteem

Children with high self-esteem are:

- ☑ Able to accept and learn from their own mistakes
- ☑ Confident without being arrogant or conceited
- ☐ Not demoralised by criticism or mild teasing
- ☑ Able to deal with their own feelings
- ☑ Less likely to be defensive when questioned
- ☐ Not easily upset by setbacks or obstacles
- ☑ Unlikely to feel a need to put others down
- ☑ Assertive but not aggressive in communicating their needs
- ☐ Not too worried about failing or looking foolish
- ☑ More likely to resist peer pressure
- ☐ Able to bounce back from disappointments and failures
- ☐ Not self-critical
- ☑ Not needing to prove themselves
- ☑ Able to take responsibility for their own happiness

- [x] Able to laugh at themselves, not taking themselves too seriously
- [x] Accepting of themselves as they are
- [x] Able to cope with change
- [ ] Generous to themselves
- [x] Generous to others
- [x] Able to accept generosity and compliments
- [x] Able to use assertive language, using statements beginning with 'I'
- [x] Able to say 'no', without offending the other person
- [x] Able to set goals for themselves and strive to reach them

Bullies avoid people with a strong sense of character, those who exude a powerful sense of self-worth. Children with high self-esteem will not feed the bully's need for power. Strengthen your child's self-esteem and the bullies will leave them alone.

Building Self-Esteem: How Can You Help Your Child?

Do things together

Without a doubt, the most effective way of improving your child's self-esteem is to spend time with him and to look for opportunities to praise his achievements. It could be while you are doing the cooking together, fixing something in the garage or pulling up the onions in the allotment.

This also gives you every opportunity to provide a role model, showing him how you look after yourself, respect and treat yourself. At this time you can make sure that he knows that you like him, that you admire his qualities and that you value his presence in the family.

For children:

self-esteem = genuine praise and reinforcement + opportunities to succeed

Catch him doing something well

This is a favourite among teachers, for changing negative behaviour into positive.

Find every opportunity to tell your child that he is doing well. Reinforce his self-esteem by giving him positive feedback wherever possible.

Examples:

- □ 'Your writing is getting better and better all the time.'
- □ 'Well done for tidying your room – you really are getting better at it.'
- □ 'Wow – I didn't know you could do that!'
- □ 'You were really kind to Jimmy. I bet that made him feel really good.'

Some tips for making him feel good about himself

- ☐ Increase family time, centred on the child's interests.
- ☐ Make sure that your mood is positive.
- ☐ Praise him in front of other people.
- ☐ Leave messages for him where he can find them privately.
- ☐ Make sure that the last thing he hears at night is a positive affirmation of his qualities, achievements and successes.
- ☐ Write a list together of all his qualities.
- ☐ Involve your child in family decisions, such as major purchases or family holidays. It will confirm to him that he is valued and important to you.
- ☐ Give him responsibilities and praise him for fulfilling them.
- ☐ Play board games together and praise him when he wins.
- ☐ Let grandparents and other relatives know how well he is doing.
- ☐ Ask him about the good things that happened at school today.
- ☐ Praise him at any time, but especially when you see him behaving in a confident manner.
- ☐ Encourage him to take risks. Limit the risks to one at a time and make sure he understands and appreciates his own success. Make them small risks at first, such as changing a routine or trying a different food (before you move on to the go-cart racing). Each risk will increase his confidence.
- ☐ Allocate regular quality time to discuss what support he needs in school or anything else.

Strengthening Self-Esteem

Visualisation

Visualisation is a very effective technique for changing your child's self-belief. This is a really powerful element of this programme, so it is worth spending some time practising this trick – and it really works. The secret to success is to really believe that you can achieve. The power of visualisation is that it convinces your subconscious mind that you can. High achievement always takes place within a framework of high expectation.

Principles of visualisation and goal-setting

These are generalised principles which work for goal-setting at any age. Children are particularly motivated by this activity, which can become an effective life-skill.

☐ Note where you are now, your situation and feelings (e.g. being bullied).

☐ Decide on your goal (e.g. self-confidence).

☐ Write down your goal and draw a picture of it, if possible.

☐ Close your eyes and have a clear image of yourself achieving the goal.

☐ Imagine yourself as if you have already achieved it.

☐ Enjoy the achievement in your imagination. Breathe it, smell it, feel it. Look at the world from your new perspective.

☐ Plan the first step towards your new goal and start straight away.

☐ When you wake up each morning, say to yourself, 'What am I going to do today towards achieving my target?' Do one thing each day and your goal will be achieved much earlier than you thought it would.

☐ Act as if your goal has already been achieved.

'The Confidence-Trick'

Stand in front of a mirror and imagine that your reflection is looking at you *from the future*. The future is a wonderful time, because you have done all of the exercises in this guide, the bullying has stopped, you feel really good about yourself and you have such wonderful self-confidence that people are amazed at how much you have changed.

Now look at the future person and see how he is standing; how his shoulders are square and straight; how he has a confident smile; and how tall he is. Take a moment to enjoy being that person. How do you feel? What does your body look like?

Enjoy being that person, because it is YOU.

Now, when you have really got into the feeling of that future person, close your eyes and imagine walking into the mirror and morphing and merging straight into your future person. **See the world from the eyes of your future person. Feel what it is like to be your future person.**

Now pinch your fingers together quite hard to 'anchor' the feeling of confidence. Pinch them harder as you imagine what it is like to be merged into your future confident person. **Remember that you only have to believe in something for it to become your reality.**

You will use the finger-pinching trick in other exercises in this guide. Each time you do a reinforcement exercise, while pinching your fingers together, it will reinforce your inner strength and confidence. Do it again now. When you need a bit of confidence, visualise your future person, pinch your thumb and first finger together and remember the good feeling. Repeat this exercise many times, until the Confidence-Trick gives you a more powerful glow of confidence every time you use it.

Affirmations

An affirmation is a key message that needs to be reinforced again and again. As the affirmation is repeated, it becomes internalised and the child gradually assimilates the message into his own subconscious. Affirmations are a very powerful way of changing internal thought patterns. They talk over the negative chatter inside our minds, and if we repeat the affirmation regularly and often enough, our subconscious and then our conscious minds gradually accept that it is so.

'As you think, so shall you be.'

Affirmations have long been accepted as a very powerful tool for changing entrenched thought patterns in adults. Children learn to use them even more quickly and easily. They enjoy pattern and repetition. The key to making the affirmations work is **repetition: so much so that you persuade your subconscious mind that they are true. By continually bombarding your subconscious with these statements, you are re-programming your mind in the most powerful way.** They can even be fitted into little corners of the day without anyone noticing.

Affirmations:

- ☐ Are written in the present tense (I am ...)
- ☐ State a deliberate intention (I feel happier all the time)
- ☐ Must not admit defeat (This probably won't work)
- ☐ Must not be conditional (If I succeed then ...)
- ☐ Must not be about anybody other than you
- ☐ Must be spoken out loud and written down
- ☐ Must be repeated time and time again

Each time you teach your child an affirmation, make sure that he is repeating it with you. The more often you both say it, the more effective it will be in empowering both of you. He will feel double the benefit. As you read the affirmation, point out the writing on the pages. This double input will increase the effectiveness even further.

Write the affirmations on sticky notes and paste them around your child's room and around the rest of the house. Get him to draw frames around them and decorate them, using symbols which relate to other interests in his life.

Together, pick out 14 affirmations, choosing the best ones to suit your child and his circumstances. Adapt them to suit your circumstances, but make sure that you keep them in the present tense, as if you are currently achieving them with a definite intention for the future. Write them down in the diary and allocate one to each day for two weeks. At the end of the two weeks, start the list again.

Examples of affirmations

- ☑ There are many things I do successfully (think of all those things you have already written down)
- ☑ I don't have to be perfect to approve of myself
- ☑ I continue to feel strong and secure inside
- ☑ I love my family and accept them as they are
- ☑ I am responsible for the decisions I make
- ☑ I am achieving my goals and ambitions
- ☑ I am a unique individual
- ☐ I find it easy to make new friends
- ☑ I am lovable
- ☒ I speak clearly and confidently ✱ *Not in front of lots of people*
- ☐ The ideas in this guide have worked for other children, so I will give them a try myself
- ☐ My self-belief grows stronger all the time
- ☐ I stay calm
- ☐ I learn quickly and easily
- ☐ I like to help others
- ☐ I'm a good person
- ☐ I finish what I start
- ☐ Every mistake I make is an opportunity to learn
- ☐ I am not afraid to make mistakes, for this is how I learn to improve
- ☐ I have the power to forgive myself for any mistakes
- ☐ I deserve support and will ask for help when I need it
- ☐ I live life with courage and confidence
- ☐ I will treat myself as someone special
- ☐ I decide what success means to me
- ☐ I feel happier all the time
- ☐ I can achieve many great things
- ☐ Challenges are exciting
- ☐ I am comfortable with who I am
- ☐ I learn new things easily
- ☐ I am developing the habit of positive thinking
- ☐ The way to make friends is to be friendly
- ☐ I don't need to play with children who are unfair

- ☐ I don't have to put up with bullying
- ☐ I have the right not to be bullied
- ☐ The world is a beautiful place
- ☐ I deserve the best
- ☐ I am strong enough to go and find something interesting to do elsewhere
- ☐ I do not rely on the good opinion of others.

A good idea is to have them move across the screen on the computer screensaver. As your child says the affirmation, do the Confidence-Trick. Do it with him and show him. Do the finger-pinching fairly hard, so that you can feel the imprint of the thumb and finger together. Repeat it again and again and again. This will add to all of the other Confidence-Trick actions in this guide and make them all the more powerful.

Remember: The Confidence-Trick anchors good feelings with a physical action. It gives your child a secret magic tool to help him when he needs a boost of self-confidence. The physical action of feeling the thumb and first finger pinching together subconsciously reminds him of his positive affirmations.

If you think that no-one will like you, then that is exactly what you will get.

If you think that everyone likes you, then that is exactly what you will get.

Do you get it?

Self-Esteem Activities

Find the good things

Adult and Child Activity

Write down four things that your child does every day which make
him feel good. This could be riding his bike home from school,
playing with a pet, reading with Mum just before he goes to sleep,
making Dad a cup of tea in the morning.

1
2
3
4

Adult and Child Activity

Now write down four more things that are *possible* within your family routines, things your child does not do at the moment but which he would like to do to make himself feel good. Agree that you will help him to do them. They could be such things as helping to make tea once a week, reading his favourite magazine together or watching a sport with Mum or Dad instead of something that he usually does on his own.

This is what I am going to do to make myself happier:

1
2
3
4

Visualisation: The golden light of confidence

Adult and Child Activity

This is a wonderful technique which your child can adapt to countless situations in his life. Make sure that he is in a peaceful space and he is warm, well fed and comfortable. Put on some restful music which will help him to become calm and relaxed.

Read this to him: Breathe deeply and slowly, trying to slow down your heart-rate.

Now close your eyes and imagine that a golden light is pouring down, through the top of your skull and working its way through your entire body. Feel this golden light of **confidence** coming down through your spine and out into your limbs.

Now imagine that the light is forming a shield around you, a wall of energy and confidence. Whatever the bully says, he can't hurt you. Even more than that, whenever the bully send nasty vibes at you – they get bounced back.

Do the Confidence-Trick, to anchor the feeling of confidence.

Repeat the exercise, using the light this time to bring you strength, and to make you relaxed. Pinch your thumb and first finger together every time, so that the Confidence-Trick becomes even more powerful.

Now use the Confidence-Trick whenever you want the golden light of confidence to pour in. No-one will notice you pinching your fingers together, but you will feel the difference.

Use this box to draw a cartoon picture of yourself with the golden confidence light pouring into you, surrounding you and forming an impenetrable shield. Choose an affirmation to put into the speech bubble:

My success bank

Child Activity

These are all the positive things people have said to me or about me this week:

| |
| |
| |
| |
| |

Remember to keep writing in the diary. There is a template for you to use at the back of this book. You could go to a discount book shop, buy a special-looking hard-backed note book and call it 'My Success Diary'. Make sure that your child only writes positive things. Occasionally read through it again together and you will be amazed at how much progress he is making.

My goals

Your child needs to have the highest expectations of himself. This exercise is designed to get him to be optimistic and to set his sights as high as possible. Goal-setting is an amazing way of increasing self-esteem. (A note of caution however: keep the goals realistic so that your child will achieve them.)

Adult and Child Activity

Write down two things you would do, if you knew you could not fail:

1
2

What would you have to do to achieve these goals?

1
2

Now choose *one* from the above list and decide how to make it come true and write it in your diary.

Do something *every* day towards making it happen.

Make a note in your diary each day to describe what you did towards your goal. You will be amazed at how quickly you meet your target.

My future diary

This is a brilliant exercise for re-programming your child's self-image.
Read this together:

Imagine that you are in the future. **All the bullying has stopped and
life is really fun.** Write an imaginary entry into your future diary
about what happened:

Dear Diary,
Today was great!

What are your future dreams?

Now think back to when you used to be bullied.

Do you really want to go back there?

I DON'T THINK SO!

Now it's time to make a commitment, to start you on the path to being

BULLY-PROOF.

Declaration

Today I have decided
that I will no longer
accept bullying
in my life.

I will do the exercises
and say the affirmations
every day for six weeks.

I dedicate this diary to

_____

because

_____

I intend to succeed and know
that you will be very proud of me

Signed _____

Anti-Bullying Strategies

It is no coincidence that strong, resourceful and confident children don't usually become the target of a bully. The last thing a bully wants is to face someone who is emotionally stronger than he is. If a bully suspects that he can intimidate someone, then that is exactly what he will try to do.

The central message of this guide is that children must assume some responsibility for stopping the bullying themselves. This skill will become invaluable to them throughout their lives. Does bullying happen only in schools? What about the workplace – even the family? The strategies and techniques involved in learning how to protect themselves will remain with them throughout their lives and will become essential life-skills.

Indeed, it is our *responsibility* to educate our children in this way. We are doing them no service by protecting them. They need to learn how to interact with all of those who would wish to prey upon their vulnerability.

Bully-Bullets

Over the next few pages is a very effective set of resources for arming your child against a bully. This is an essential section, because once your child is beginning to strengthen his self-esteem, he will be ready to face the bully with a new-found confidence. Now he needs to learn how to:

Baffle the Bully

The trick is to use a 'Bully-bullet' to redress the balance in a potential bullying situation. Given a little practice, it will become a very effective part of your child's arsenal against a bully who teases.

The next few pages are directed straight to your child. They contain essential anti-bully 'bullets'. It is worth spending a lot of time understanding and learning how to use these resources. These tricks work.

Check through the table on the next page, and in the spaces write down the phrases which a bully might have used against your child, e.g. 'you're so fat', 'four-eyes', etc.

Look at the Bully-bullets and agree which ones would work for your child. Change the responses if you wish, using language which is natural to your child and your culture. Practise time and time again, within the security of the family, before unleashing the new skill on the bully.

Turn it into a game, learning how to use 'banter' to take the sting out of a possibly confrontational situation.

When practising the replies, always use clear, calm, slow and confident speech; make eye contact, stand tall and *always* walk away.

Once your child can use a quick retort in a game, get him to try it out on the bully. Watch the bully become very confused – he won't expect to be answered back.

Bully's taunts (fill in the spaces)	Bully-bullets
You're fat	Well thank you for that. You're so kind. I'm clever too.
We don't want you to play with us	Well thanks for letting me know; I can play with ………. then. Now where is he?
I don't like you	Well it's a waste of my time playing with you then …
We don't want you in our group	Oh good. I can go and make some new friends then.
	You used that tease last week. Can't you think of a new one?
	I've got better things to do than try to make friends with a bully.
	I really appreciate your feedback.
	Oh dear – how sad – never mind.
	Where's your evidence?
	I know, but why? (baffle him)
	I know you'd like me to be like you, but thankfully, I am an individual.
	Did you know that the way to make friends is to be friendly?
	I know you like teasing me, but please push off and try it on someone else – I'm too busy at the moment to deal with you. Try again tomorrow afternoon perhaps?

and some more …

Bully's taunts (fill in the spaces)	Bully-bullets
You're………	I hope you won't keep boring me with this remark every time I see you.
	True, but I am a genius.
	Try that again and I'll report you to …
	If you stop being irritating, I might not report you this time.
	Thank you for this training in how to look after myself.
	Thank you for teaching me how to deal with a bully.
	I've got better things to do than try to make friends with a bully.
	I think you've read the wrong book on how to make friends.
	If you carry on [*name the bullying activity*] then I will have to decide who to report you to. I already have your parents, my parents, the headteacher and the police on my list. Yes, I think it's about time.
	This bullying isn't working. Do you think that you need a bit more practice?
	Where's your evidence?
	I know – aren't I lucky?
	Yes, I've taken years to perfect this technique.
	Yes I am – are you jealous?

Now have fun making up some of your own. You get the idea – be assertive, without being rude; baffle the bully with your intelligent Bully-bullets and generally turn the encounter into a positive one, *in which the bully is doing you a favour*. Practise with someone at home until the replies become second nature. Then it's time to unleash your new-found Bully-bullet skills on the bully. Won't he be surprised? He won't know what to do. He will be expecting you to react by being upset, which is exactly what he wants. Remember that a bully is usually a coward, and will not want to stick around if he is not getting the response he wants – he'll move off and try to find someone else. Watch it happening and make sure that you write your successes down in your Success Diary – exactly what he said and how you replied. The trick will come to you even more easily the next time – and so on.

Make sure that your Bully-bullet is POSITIVE and lets the bully know that what he is saying is going to lead to a GOOD thing happening for you.

Choose one Bully-bullet at a time to practise – don't try them all at once, or the task will become too much for you and you'll give up.

Practise the Bully-bullets, talking to an empty chair, or your teddy bear. (It works.) You may feel a bit silly, but does it matter? You won't be feeling silly once you are in a Bully-Free Zone.

A bagful of Bully-bullets

If you use a mixture of replies, the bully will be utterly confused. He will not be getting his predicted response and will leave you alone, in order to go and find someone easier to bully. All this takes a little practice to become part of your normal language, but it is fun practising it with friends and family. Don't try to learn all of them. Just choose two or three that you feel comfortable with. Once you start getting a result you will want to try more. Bullies beware. So here we go with some more Bully-bullet ideas.

- ☐ Surprise the bully by agreeing with him. This takes away his power: 'Well thank you for your comments – they really help'; 'Thank you for telling me that – how sweet of you to notice.'
- ☐ Shock them by behaving very differently: pretend to vomit in front of them, sing the National Anthem or laugh really loudly at them.
- ☐ Draw attention to them by shouting within earshot of an adult: 'I don't think you should be bullying me.' They are less likely to bully you again if you embarrass them.
- ☐ Interrupt them and start talking about something completely different – make sure that it is something positive. Use disconnected comments such as 'This is such a fun game, isn't it?'
- ☐ Challenge them by asking questions: 'Exactly who said that you could try to bully me like this?' Keep asking them questions and engaging them in conversation.
- ☐ Clarify what they are saying to you: 'So what is it that you don't like about me again?'
- ☐ Ask them directly what they are trying to do: 'Are you trying to hurt my feelings or are you trying to be my friend?'
- ☐ Match their anger with your sympathy: 'I understand why you are so upset and I would do exactly the same if I were you, but …'
- ☐ Baffle them with a confusing reply: 'I know – but why is it green?'

- [ ] Use short responses, if you can't think of an immediate reply: 'Great', 'OK then', 'So what?', 'Well I never!', 'Whatever!', 'You're so right.'
- [ ] Use the visualisation tricks: pretend to yourself that the bully's taunt is something physical, like a ball kicked at you, which you can dodge, or a laser beam which is deflected because of your force-field. A very good trick is to imagine that you have a mirror force-field, which deflects the bully's attack straight back at him.

Fact: It's OK to make mistakes. Nobody's perfect.

When a Bully Taunts You
- [ ] Here are some ways to protect yourself when a bully taunts you:
- [ ] Look at the bully, straight into his eyes
- [ ] Don't get upset or let the bully know how you feel
- [ ] Stand still – don't wriggle about
- [ ] Maintain a blank, neutral look on your face
- [ ] Check your stance – are you standing straight up, with your shoulders straight and square? Imagine that a string is attached to the top of your skull and is pulling you up to the sky
- [ ] Speak clearly, loudly, slowly and calmly
- [ ] Use one of the Bully-bullets that you have practised
- [ ] Go straight to a person in authority (parent or teacher) and tell them exactly what has just happened
- [ ] Write the incident down in your diary during the evening, including the names of any witnesses
- [ ] Ask Mum when you can start karate lessons.

Fact: YOU are NOT responsible for anyone else or their feelings.

How to Combat Mobile Phone Bullying

This disturbing recent phenomenon has taken bullying to a new and frightening level. An ever-increasing number of children own mobile phones and there is no doubt that parents feel more secure knowing that they have direct contact with their children. However, until the telecommunications providers sort out the security issues surrounding the anonymity of Pay-As-You-Go mobile phones, our children are vulnerable to this perverse form of harassment. Statistics published in 2006 by the children's charity, National Children's Home (NCH), showed that 25% of students had been threatened in chat rooms or by e-mail, and 16% had been bullied by text message.

If your child is bullied in this way, he should:

- ☐ Tell you straight away.
- ☐ Never ignore mobile phone threats, but treat this as a very serious matter.
- ☐ Not respond. The bully is trying to control him, and by responding, he is giving him exactly what he wants. It will make him do it all the more.
- ☐ Keep the message as evidence.
- ☐ Keep a detailed diary of the date, time, caller-ID or the 'unavailable' message.
- ☐ Print off the messages if possible.
- ☐ If possible, buy him a Pay-As-You-Go phone and ensure that he only gives the number to family and trusted friends.
- ☐ Give the mobile phone on which he is receiving threatening messages to the police. It will be gratifying to you to know that the bully is texting the police station.
- ☐ Know that in making these threats, accusations, etc, the bully is revealing his own shortcomings and weaknesses.
- ☐ Think through the list of people who might be doing it as your child very probably knows the person who is sending these calls and messages. They are probably jealous of your child and they certainly feel insecure.

What to Do About Girls' Cliques

One of the most distressing forms of bullying, especially for a girl, is where another girl or group of girls decide to ostracise her and exclude her from the group.

All humans need to belong to a group to one extent or another, but young girls seem to need the support of their friends more than any other group. In our modern society the need to 'belong to the tribe' is as strong as ever. The child who is insecure or lacking in self-esteem needs the support of peers even more and is thus extremely vulnerable to the effects of exclusion.

If your child is being excluded by members of her group, she should:

- ☐ Make sure that an adult knows exactly what is happening. Ask a teacher to watch out for the excluding behaviour.
- ☐ Try approaching each member of the group individually and pointing out to them what is happening. This type of meanness has probably happened to everyone in the group, so they will all know what it feels like.
- ☐ Realise that this will give her opportunities for new friendships. Even though she may not feel like it at the moment, this situation really does give her a chance to find new friends. Think about it – are her existing 'friends' being kind to her? Are they really 'friends'? Is there someone else who might be more loyal and more of a true friend?
- ☐ Ask her drama teacher to devise a role-play about excluding behaviour and its impact.
- ☐ Make sure that she has more than one group of friends and avoids having just one 'best friend'.
- ☐ Not share sensitive personal information which a 'friend' could use to turn against her.
- ☐ Join a club outside school, to increase her social circle.
- ☐ Do some 'spring-cleaning'. Ditch the friendship group which takes it in turns to exclude one member at a time. They are revealing their own insecurities. Find a more stable group of friends.

- ☐ Choose some 'fun' friends. Surrounding herself with moody miseries will only drag her down. Better to seek out the ones who are laughing and enjoying themselves.
- ☐ Try not to run her life according to what other people think of her. 'Marching to your own drummer' means being an individual – she will gain more respect in the long run. We don't need other people's approval.
- ☐ Avoid gossiping herself. It's really tempting to join in, but only those people with a low self-worth need to 'rubbish' others to make themselves feel good. It also damages self-esteem, and causes guilt inside. When someone frequently judges others, they are just demonstrating that they are a person who needs to judge. **You can be sure that the person who is leading the 'bitching' is the most insecure one in the group**.

Sometimes, the taunts and gossip contain a grain of truth, which will make your daughter feel uncomfortable. None of us are perfect and this 'grain of truth' tactic is meant to make her feel powerless. The message is: 'Don't fall for it'. Perfect people must be very boring.

If someone is unpleasant enough to cut her out of their play, does she really want them as a friend? Will she always be able to trust them? If she can't find someone to play with, she can look at it as an opportunity to go and spend some time with herself.

How to Be Happy (1)

Go through the following 'happy tips' with your child, decide which ones you like best and put them in the diary.

- [ ] As you put your head on your pillow at night, look forward to the next few minutes of thinking of all the best things that could possibly happen to you. No-one can spoil this moment, because it is private and only you know about it.
- [ ] Wear strongly coloured clothes.
- [ ] When you find a negative thought creeping into your head, say 'OUT!' and boot it out into space. You may like to go somewhere private and actually act it out.
- [ ] Expect the BEST to happen to you and it will happen. (By the way, if you expect the WORST – that will happen too.) Your subconscious is so powerful that what it expects will happen, will usually do so. If you expect happiness, then you will attract happiness.
- [ ] Smile at people – see the result.
- [ ] Be generous with your compliments.
- [ ] Take your dog (or someone else's) for a walk. Spend some time stroking a furry animal and feel the softness of its coat.
- [ ] Keep fit. Using energy up in physical fitness creates even more energy. Powerful chemicals are released in your body while you are exercising and for a long time afterwards. They work every time, don't have any after-effects and improve your health.
- [ ] Have a joke book at hand. Tell a really funny one to the cat or dog. Have a joke a day to tell your friends. They will seek you out. Everyone likes a friend with a smiley face – you will be very popular.

How to Cope with an Angry Bully

Older Child Activity

Older children will learn an essential life-skill if they can practise this technique:

- ☐ Be calm and listen carefully.
- ☐ Say to yourself that his anger belongs to him – it isn't yours and he's probably having a go at you because he has a problem and you got in the way. You don't have to take it personally.
- ☐ Listen to what he is saying and watch what he is doing.
- ☐ Look for an opportunity to speak and use his name politely – it calms him down enough for you to interrupt.
- ☐ Use your hand in a 'stop' sign.
- ☐ At first, speak as loudly as he is doing, but then straight away lower your voice until it is really low and calm. If you practise this, it will become a tool which you can use for the rest of your life.
- ☐ Say, 'I understand that you are angry.'
- ☐ Repeat back to him what he has just said: 'So you are saying that …' This takes the sting out of his anger and shows that actually you do understand him. Bullies don't expect to be 'understood'.
- ☐ Respect yourself by saying that you disagree, if this is so, but say it calmly, after you have told him that you understand why he is angry.
- ☐ Stand straight and square; stay tall and confident. Say, 'see you later' and just walk away. Don't get involved and don't let his anger rub off on you. Respect yourself.

Dealing with angry people is a life-skill. Everybody gets angry sometimes and you will gain a lot of respect if you can stay calm.

How to Manage Your Own Anger

Older Child Activity

Of course, sometimes, you will feel angry too. Sometimes being bullied results in some very negative feelings, including anger. Here is a very good way to calm down, in a way that no-one else is aware of:

- ☐ Breathe slowly, counting to ten.
- ☐ Hold this breath for a count of five.
- ☐ Think of a situation in which you were really happy. Imagine you're on holiday, in the pool, floating on a lilo, looking up at the sky.
- ☐ Try to hold that feeling.
- ☐ Exhale slowly for a count of ten. (You can do it.)
- ☐ Count to five before you breathe in again.
- ☐ Repeat this cycle a few times.
- ☐ You should now feel more calm and in control.
- ☐ Now think carefully about your choice as to what to do next. You can either get involved or walk away.
- ☐ What is the best thing to do right now?

Is getting angry going to improve the situation?

No? Good choice.

Whenever you allow yourself to feel anger, you feel weaker for the effort. Save your energy. Walk away and look for something positive to channel your energies into. Conflict cannot survive without your participation.

How to Release Negative Feelings

Child Activity

- ☐ Hit a punch bag or a cushion.
- ☐ Do some physical exercise – something which you really like. It could be running, skipping or kicking a football – whatever you want.
- ☐ Play music loudly. Dance to the music – this is a wonderful way to release feelings and end up feeling really good about yourself. Use headphones if your music would disturb someone else.

Keep a diary about how you feel. Always end your diary entry by writing down one really good thing which happened to you today, naming one person who helped you or made you happy. This will help you to see the positive side of life and to look forward to writing in your diary again.

Squeeze a stress-ball or piece of plasticene.

Ideas of your own (make sure that they are assertive and positive, but not aggressive):
My idea for releasing anger:
My idea for releasing fear:
My idea for releasing sadness:
Other feelings I want to release:

How to Say 'No'

Saying 'No' is something that many of us find difficult. It is even more difficult for a child who is naturally quiet or shy, especially in the face of a bully who is intent on exerting his power.

The key is to realise that it is our **right** to say 'No' and that it is perfectly acceptable to do so.

Try this:

Look the other person in the eye. Make sure that the first word you use is 'No'.

Say something like:

- ☐ No, I am not comfortable with that
- ☐ No, I am in the middle of something
- ☐ No, I don't enjoy that
- ☐ No, I was just about to go and do something else
- ☐ No, it wouldn't leave me any time to play
- ☐ No, try and find someone else to do it for you

Don't offer to help the other person out.

Don't say 'sorry'.

Don't make excuses.

It is your right to say 'No'.

If all else fails – walk away.

How to Improve Body Language

It is worth spending time working on your child's body language. His posture will reveal his inner confidence in a way that a hundred words would not.

Assertive standing involves standing straight and 'thinking tall', as if an invisible thread is joined to the top of his head and is pulling him upwards. Feet need to be planted firmly on the ground with the body square on, using up as much 'space' as possible.

Matching and mirroring the other's body language (without being a copy-cat) can reduce the tension between two children. For instance, if one child is leaning on a wall, then 'matching' the body language would mean that the other child would be leaning too.

Child Activity

When speaking to someone who might be trying to gain power over you, remember to tell yourself that you are as worthy as the other person.

If you believe in yourself, it will show in your body language and other people will believe in you too.

Use one of these affirmations:

- ☐ 'I have great confidence in myself.'
- ☐ 'I am a good person.'
- ☐ 'My bully-proof shield is activated.'

Body language exercise: 'Don't even think about it!'

Child Activity

Stand or sit facing a mirror, thinking about a time when you have been bullied.

Look at your face. Are your eyes shining and bright, or are you looking down or sideways? Are your lips tight or is your mouth open and smiley?

Look at your shoulders. Are they slumped over or pulled back and straight?

Say 'hello' to yourself (go on – I know it sounds silly). What is your voice like – small, quiet, muffled, grunting – or loud and confident?

Look again at yourself. This is the person that the bully is seeing. Is your body language going to tell the bully that he is succeeding? Do you want them to come back again? I don't think so.

Now let's change that body language. Imagine that you are strong, invincible. Let's tell that cowardly bully – 'Don't even think about it!'

Think of a time when you have done something really well, when you have been particularly successful. Perhaps it was a time when your teacher praised you in front of the class and it made you feel really good. Perhaps it was when you learned to swim or ride a bike. Hold that feeling now. What does it feel like? Look at your body language this time. Make sure that you are standing tall – even taller. Are your eyes twinkling? Is there a happy confident smile on your lips? Or a quiet determination perhaps?

Now this is the best bit. Look into the mirror at the bully. Not scared of him now, are you? Look hard at him and *think to yourself*, 'Don't even think about it'.

Now you must *practise* that look and that feeling. Make the message come out of your eyes. Tell the mirror, with your eyes and facial expression, 'Don't even think about it!' Now make eye contact with the bully, stand tall and walk away.

Do this exercise time and time again, so that your body knows exactly what to do when a bully comes up to you. The bully will recognise instantly that you are different and it will make him uncertain and less brave.

Cartoon picture of me saying, 'Don't even think about it!'

Body language exercise: keeping eye contact

Maintaining eye contact in our culture and society shows that you have inner strength. It demonstrates self-assurance, and when you look straight into a person's eyes it makes you look more confident.

The child who avoids eye contact may just not have learned this particular social skill, but he will be at a disadvantage until he does.

For those parents who may have exhausted the record, 'Look at me when I talk to you,' here is a fun way to play the eye contact game.

Use a glove puppet and move it to wherever your child is looking, so that it looks as if he is talking to the puppet.

It always gets a laugh and you end up with a smiley child who is also looking into your eyes.

Soon, you will only have to grab the puppet for the exercise to be reinforced.

Maintaining eye contact with the bully is essential

Other games include staring competitions, pretending that your eyes are laser-destroyers.

Body language exercise: get the look

Not only should you maintain eye contact, but you need to remember that your eyes reflect what you are saying 'on the inside'.

Child Activity

Practise in front of a mirror 'saying' things with your eyes only.

Try these:

- ☐ How very interesting
- ☐ I'm bored with this conversation
- ☐ How amazing – I'm stunned!
- ☐ How long is this going to take?
- ☐ I am a cloud
- ☐ DON'T EVEN THINK ABOUT IT!

Hold the look until it becomes a stare. It's really good fun. Look into a mirror and try the 'Heavyweight Champion of the World' look, or the Catherine Tate 'Am I bovver'd?' look. What you need to do is make sure that you do NOT show your true feelings. The bully wants to have an effect on you. If you give him what he wants he will come back time and time again. If you don't, then he will go elsewhere. Remember, we are making sure that you are not the victim of the bully.

Have a staring match with your friend and see if you can identify what the other person is thinking.

Remember that the bully has no right to know what you are feeling inside. Keep him guessing by hiding your true feelings from him. Practise this until you are really good at it.

Body language collage

Adult and Child Activity

This is really good fun and helps you to be aware of the power of body language.

You need:

- ☐ old children's magazines
- ☐ large sheet of paper
- ☐ scissors
- ☐ glue stick

Look through the magazines for examples of children standing or sitting in an assertive way. Notice their eyes and their body posture.

Cut out the ones which appeal to you and look like pictures of children who are especially confident.

Stick them onto a collage and pin it onto the wall in your room.

Now stand in front of the picture and imagine that you are all of those children put together.

Feel how much confidence you have. How are you standing? Is your head being pulled up to the ceiling by that imaginary string? Absorb their confidence and close your eyes, keeping that confidence inside you.

Now, while doing the Confidence-Trick, step into the picture and become those confident children. See the world from their eyes. Feel what they feel. Open your eyes and enjoy the feeling of confidence and power.

Whenever you need a bit of confidence, pinch your thumb and first finger together and remind yourself of how powerful you really are.

Body language exercise: using a video camera

Adult and Child Activity

This is a really useful exercise for pointing out how crucial body language is for keeping bullies at bay.

Get a favourite poem, song or rhyme, learn a few lines and video yourself saying or singing it.

Now, using the Confidence-Trick, project yourself into the most confident person that you know. It could be a film star, a TV presenter, a friend or a member of your family.

Now say or sing the poem again, but this time pretend to be the confident person and act as if you are them. Watch both video clips and note down:

	Before	After
How did I stand: up straight/hunched over, etc?		
What expression did I have on my face?		
How did I speak/sing? Calmly, quickly, slowly, etc.?		
What differences were there in my eyes?		
Other differences:		

Now write down one aspect of your body language that you can focus on to change:

Every day for one week, notice how that particular aspect of your body language is behaving.

Now repeat the exercise and focus on the next aspect of your body language to change. Make it a fun exercise by choosing entertaining poems or songs to film.

How to Change Faulty Beliefs

One of the ways we can change our beliefs is to change the language we use to describe ourselves. Instead of using destructive self-talk, we can re-phrase our statements in a positive way. This instructs our subconscious to re-frame our view of ourselves. Children understand this concept really easily if it is played as a game.

Adult and Child Activity

Try changing your faulty beliefs into positive beliefs like this (fill in some of your own ideas in the empty rows):

Existing faulty belief	New positive belief
I am different from others and people don't like me	I am glad that I am different and that makes me very lovable
I deserve to be bullied because I am no good at anything	I understand why I have been bullied, but that's going to stop now
Nobody will ever stop the bullying	The ideas in this guide have worked for other children, and they are going to work for me too

Try to catch yourself using negative self-talk and play a game of re-framing your language in a positive way.

Tip: One person may see a half-glass of water as being 'half-full' when another person would describe it as 'half-empty'. Try to encourage your child to view the world through the eyes of a 'half-full' person.

How to write your own creed

A creed is a very effective way of building an inner belief system.

Once you have written it, try to make it into a rhyme, or even put it to music, like the rhymes that soldiers sing when they're jogging. Make sure that it's all positive and that it is stated in the present tense with a future intention, e.g., 'I believe that I am getting more confident every day'.

Of course, the secret, as with the rest of this guide, is to *practise* what you have written.

I believe that I

_____

I believe that I

_____

I believe that

_____

I believe that I

_____

I believe that I

_____

How to Be Happy (2)

☐ At night time, give your worries to a worry-doll who will look after them during the night – you will feel much better in the morning.

☐ Make a habit of telling people only your good news, not the bad news. It will make other people feel happy and they will look forward to seeing you again.

☐ Don't use up all your energy listening to 'needy' friends. Yes, you understand how they feel, but your mood could be dragged down at a time when you really need it to be boosted up.

☐ 'Life is what happens while you are making other plans,' said John Lennon. Concentrate on the present and don't worry about the past. You can't do anything about the past, no matter how good or bad it was. It's gone. Neither can you affect the future by worrying about it. If anything, worrying will drain your energy and it will not have the slightest effect on what happens.

☐ If you find yourself criticising another person, stop and say something constructive and complimentary instead.

☐ You don't always have to be right. Sometimes it's best just to choose to be kind, even though you know the other person is in the wrong.

☐ Ask Mum to give you a massage.

☐ Choose an affirmation from your Affirmation List and have fun telling it to yourself ten times every morning and night for a week. Then choose another one.

How to Make Friends

A message to a Bully (of any age):

We all need friends.

The message could not be clearer: the way to make friends is to be friendly.

You may feel that you need to exert power over others and that you will gain respect this way. If you understand this message right now, you will save yourself from a lifetime of loneliness. What you are doing by bullying is achieving the exact opposite of what you want. You are demonstrating that you are lacking in character; you are losing the respect of others and you could find it very difficut to get it back. **But this needn't be so**.

If you want power, please realise that you can have the most awesome power by helping other children to feel good about themselves – how much better does that feel? Walk down the corridor and say hello to one of your previous victims, using their name, smiling with a genuine concern for their happiness. Ask them about their lives. See how many friends you start to gather this way. Today, you could use your power to change a victim into a friend. What an incredible opportunity you have!

The kind of person who attracts friends is unselfish and giving, and always puts being kind above the need for personal gain. Learn this really important message now and change from being a bully into a friend-magnet. **Good luck**.

If you know a bully, photocopy this page and give it to them straight! The world will be a better place with one less bully. In this day and age, bullying should not be happening to your child. He doesn't deserve it. Let's do what we can to stop it right now.

If your child is a bully then it is likely that his behaviour stems from poor self-esteem. He needs support as much as the victimdoes . He also needs to follow this guide and start making true friends.

More Essential Anti-Bullying Tips and Tricks

☐ Don't show the bully you are upset, but do tell him that his behaviour is unacceptable. It's none of his business how you feel. Show your true feelings to your family instead. Bullies love a reaction – don't give them one. If you show the bully that you are upset, then you are rewarding his aggression and it may be exactly what he wants to hear to give him a feeling of power.

☐ Do keep your head up. Tilting your head to one side is a show of submission. Face the bully. Don't look down or sideways. Look straight at him and let your eyes say, 'Don't even think about it!'

☐ Make eye contact, stand tall and walk away. Practise this in front of the mirror, say it to the dog, confront the goldfish and surprise your Auntie Flossie, but make sure that you practise it.

☐ If a bully is throwing things at you in class, keep all of the objects until you can show the collection to the teacher.

☐ If someone is stealing things from you or moving your stuff, then report it to a teacher and ask if they can keep a watch out to catch the bully red-handed.

☐ If someone physically hurts you, then tell him or her that you are about to report them and go and do just that.

☐ Bullying usually occurs where there is very little adult supervision, so make sure that you identify these areas (e.g. toilets or locker areas) and avoid them. Stay where you know there is supervision.

☐ Don't hit back or abuse them back, even if you have been encouraged to do so by friends or well-meaning family. If you do, you will find that you are in as much trouble as they are.

☐ If your intuition, your gut instinct, tells you that you are in danger, don't hang around, but get away as soon as possible. Try to baffle the bully, and distract him in order to escape, before going straight to find an adult to help you.

☐ Take up karate, tai chi, yoga or judo. It does wonders for your self-esteem and it means that you can repel an attack without being aggressive.

- [ ] If you want to say 'no', say 'no', calmly and firmly. Don't make excuses or try to offer the other person an alternative. Use a strong tone of voice and maintain firm eye contact.
- [ ] Beware of taking up too little space. Use up as much space as you can. Stand tall and square, not hunched up.
- [ ] Don't take expensive items to school. Envy is a major trigger for a bully.
- [ ] Telling a teacher: If your teacher has dismissed your problem in the past because they have been too busy, say this: 'I need to talk to you in private. When could you give me ten minutes of your time?' Make sure that you take with you anything which you have written down about the problem. Ask his/her advice. Say that you really want to do well at school, but that the problem with the bully is preventing you from concentrating and learning. If the teacher still does not listen, get your parents to write to the headteacher, the Chair of Governors and the Local Education Authority (there are some example letters at the end of this book).

If an adult bullies you by trying to get you to do something you are not comfortable with, then you need to get help immediately. Tell someone you trust or ring Childline: 0800 1111.

Action Plans

Action plan: bullying

Child Activity

Write down all of the ways in which bullies try to upset you. Now go back through this guide and decide how you are going to deal with each of them. Choose the best response which will work for you. Don't use all of your ideas in one go. Use the 'drip-feed' approach. Deflate the bully bit by bit and it will give you even more confidence. This is your action plan.

One month later, look at this list again. Does the plan need to change?

How the bully upsets me	What I am going to do about it

Now go back through the book, using a highlighting pen, making a note of things you need to remember in your diary.

Action plan: how to be happy

Child Activity

Go through the 'How to be happy' tips and write down the ones which work best for you. Re-visit the list and make changes, or re-write them using your own language:

My favourite happy tips:

Action plan: favourite affirmations

Child Activity

Now do the same for your favourite affirmations. Change the language to suit your style.

My favourite affirmations:

Action plan: favourite Bully-bullets

Child Activity

Now do the same for your favourite Bully-bullets. Again, change the language so it better suits your style.

My favourite Bully-bullets:

Oh, what are we going to do?

Your friend is being bullied. Using what you have learned in this guide, can you give him your six best anti-bully tips to stop him from being bullied?	
1.	2.
3.	4.
5.	6.

Final Checklist

- [ ] If you are bullied, it is not your fault. You don't deserve to be bullied – ever.
- [ ] Accept, however, that you can be largely responsible for keeping the bully away from you.
- [ ] Decide that you have been bullied for the last time – from now on things are getting better.
- [ ] Decide that you are going to practise and practise and practise the techniques described in this guide.
- [ ] Get used to saying affirmations as a way of improving your self-worth and determination to succeed.
- [ ] Learn the Confidence-Trick and use it whenever you need a bit of confidence.
- [ ] Get fit and gain the respect of your peers.
- [ ] If you don't feel confident inside, then 'fake it'. After a while it will become part of your behaviour and you won't need to pretend any more. If you appear confident, then people are going to notice and appreciate you – and you will inspire trust and confidence in others.
- [ ] Master the use of the blank, neutral look.
- [ ] Remember that it is the bully who has the problem – not you. You don't need to let them drag you down to their low level.
- [ ] Learn and practise some of the Bully-bullets in this guide and make them part of your vocabulary.
- [ ] Get your body language right. Always make eye contact, stand tall, smile and walk away.
- [ ] Keep away from low-energy people – that means make sure that you surround yourself with the kind of people who have high self-esteem. If you find yourself spending time with a negative person or a moaner, then deliberately move away and find someone who is happy and who will raise your spirits.
- [ ] Don't criticise yourself. It reduces your energy and will only drag you down. If you make a mistake, say to yourself that mistakes are the necessary stepping-stones to learning and success. We all have to make mistakes and there's nothing wrong with that. The trick is to make sure that you don't keep making

the same mistakes over and over again. The biggest mistake you can make in life is to be continually worrying about making one. There is a wonderful quotation from James Joyce, who said, 'mistakes are the portals of discovery'.

☐ Keep a diary and record events and feelings.

☐ When negative thoughts creep in, say 'Hello' to the thought as if it is a visitor, then 'Goodbye', then 'Out!' to yourself and feel your brain kicking them out of your head. Then pinch your thumb and first finger together and remind yourself of your positive strengths. Say your favourite affirmation and know that you are strong. This might take a bit of practice, but it is so effective if you persevere with it and the technique will remain with you all of your life. **People who are positive thinkers attract friends – those who are negative send them away.**

☐ Give yourself some happy time and find ways to feel good about yourself.

Every moment that you spend being upset or angry because of someone else's behaviour, that is a moment in which you have given up control of your life to the other person. The bully is controlling your life. He is the one with the problem – it is not yours. You do not need the friendship of this person – he is draining you and controlling your life. You will become a non-victim as soon as you stop expecting to be victimised.

Appendices

Diary of Events

Name of Child:

Date of incident:	Place:
Bully's name:	Witnesses:
Description of incident:	
Reported to:	Resolved/unresolved:
Action taken:	Follow up:

Name of Child:

Date of incident:	Place:
Bully's name:	Witnesses:
Description of incident:	
Reported to:	Resolved/unresolved:
Action taken:	Follow up:

Letter to the School

[Name of headteacher]

[School address and postcode]

Dear [Name of Headteacher]

Re: [Name of child]

Thank you for seeing me yesterday about [name of child].

If you recall, I was concerned about the following incident/s which has/have happened in school:

We agreed to

You said you would monitor the situation and

Please can we have a meeting in two weeks' time, to discuss the situation further?

Please put a copy of this letter onto my child's file and let me have a copy of the school's bullying policy.

Yours sincerely,

Letter to the Chair of Governors

[Your address]

[Date]

To: Chair of Governors

[Name of school]

[Address of school]

Dear Chair of Governors,

Re: Bullying of [name of child]

Having contacted the school regarding the bullying of my child, I am disappointed that the bullying issues have not yet been resolved and that the bullying is still taking place.

Please would you:

- [ ] let me know when I can meet you to discuss this problem
- [ ] put bullying on the agenda for the next Governors' Board meeting

I await your urgent response.

Yours faithfully,

[Your name]

Diary Pages

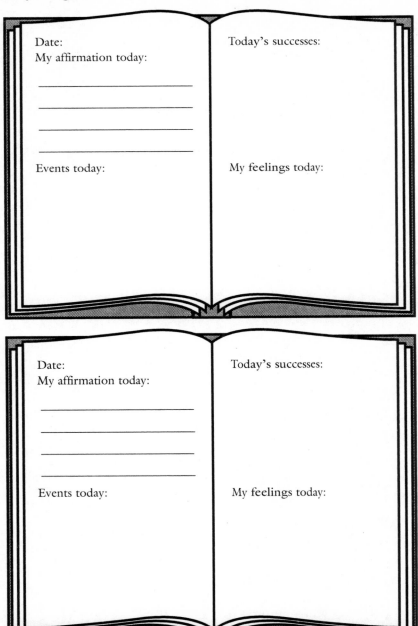

Date:
My affirmation today:

Today's successes:

_____

_____

_____

_____

Events today:

My feelings today:

Date:
My affirmation today:

Today's successes:

_____

_____

_____

_____

Events today:

My feelings today:

Aladdin's Cave of Recommended Links

www.childline.org.uk

www.met.police.uk/youth/bullying.htm

www.barnardos.org.uk

www.the-childrens-society.org.uk

www.nspcc.org.uk

www.kidscape.org.uk

www.bullyonline.org

http://www.parentscentre.gov.uk/educationandlearning/schoollife/ifthingsgowrong/bullyingproblems/

http://www.dfes.gov.uk/bullying/

Visit Coral online at www.neverbullied.com

Supported Charity

The following charity is supported by this publication:

The National Bullying Helpline (Charity No. 117852)